The Quick Guide to Selling Your Business

by Huzeifa Anjary

Special thanks to:

Vincent Doherty MA MA(ED)

Idris Anjary BA (Hons) PgDip Arch

Printed and bound by Lulu

ISBN 978-1-4717-1855-7

"He who perseveres patiently will not be deprived of success, no matter how long it takes." *Ali i'bne Abi Taalib(AS) 600AD*

Dedicated to my parents

Contents

About the Author

From a very young age I was whisked into business and have never looked back.

Starting with a low budget start-up I now own and run two franchises. Having been directly and indirectly involved in the sales of several business and franchises, I discovered that there was a pattern and that, simply put, I was good at selling businesses. Whether it was my own or another's, I could sell any business.

I looked at businesses as complete products and found the day to day running of a business was not what excited me. This is the main reason I went into franchising and now own and run CareGREEN, which deals with solar and eco related franchises, and Sonic Print, which sells print franchises.

I have found a strategy that has worked time and again. Not only can it be used to sell successful, operating businesses but also ones that didn't work or were closing down. I found that a successful sale had very little to do with the business itself and more to do with how you went about selling it.

Therefore, this book offers you **The Quick Way** to sell your business at the best possible price, in the best possible time.

I wish you every success,

Huzeifa Anjary

Introduction

I have often wondered what it is that makes one person successful and another one fail. Is it down to genes or education? Is it just luck or cosmic disturbances or destiny? Some believe it is the power of the Almighty that determines success; others even say it is the power of the human mind and your self-belief. It might as well be all the above because the one thing I have found in business is that there is no one answer.

Have you heard the tale of the pound storyteller? 'I came to town with nothing but a single pound in my pocket and now I am very successful'. What was it that they had? Surely not the fact that they started skint? The answer is no, all they had to make them rich was an all-important self-belief and that **will** to become somebody. To be successful.

I have compiled this book out of my own experience and that of my father – to whom I owe a great deal as he is the one who took my hand and led me onto the path of business. More importantly, he served as a great role model. From owning a construction company in a far-flung corner of the earth employing over 300 men, to determinedly working on his own, he showed me that, through success or failure, one thing is for sure, to be in business is to be strong-willed and determined !

If you are looking to sell your business then you will find this book invaluable. I will prove that you can sell your business quickly and effectively, at (or pretty near) your intended asking price and the only tool you will need is determination and **will**.

Chapter 1: You

1. Why this book is for you

Whether you work for yourself and are classed as self employed, pay Class X national contributions , or pay corporation tax, then you are in business. Your business may be classified as a limited company or partnership, sole trader or public registered. However you class yourself, if your business has now reached a point where you are saying to yourself, 'Enough is enough I want out!'; or age or health now restrict you from running the show; or a partnership is now ending as partners want to move off in their own direction; or other personal circumstances are influencing you; whatever the cause the result is the same. **You need to sell your business in the shortest possible time and get the maximum amount for it.**

For this to happen successfully you must have the **will** to be, to do and to become and this book will hopefully inspire you to sell your business with the use of some simple formulas I have learnt over the years. On completing this book you will know what to do to set up the selling process, what to do during the sale, and how to become a successful seller.

2. Experience

It is wise to listen to experiences from the horse's mouth and there are a lot of my own experiences in this book as someone who has chosen both the right and wrong paths in the past. Some methods just work, they have little or no failure rate, others are complete 'dead ends'. It may be that what you are doing is just right, but not enough. This book will guide you through a step-by-step process after which any business will fetch a better price.

I started out in business very early on. After my A-levels I attended a course in Architectural Design with my brother, who later went on to become an architect. No sooner had we completed the course than my father sat us down to draw up a plan and a business model to complete a high-rise building. We were learning about business the practical way, without any knowledge of the logistics involved in such a venture, but this proved to be the advantage. Because we did not know, we just jumped straight in.

It was only after we jumped that we realised the depth, but since we were in we swam on. Before anyone could say, 'What?' or 'How?', we had designed and prepared a complete feasibility study of the costings and planning consents for a high-rise skyscraper in Asia. We were in our early 20s at the time and talking to major financiers who were treating us seriously. Why were they even listening to us? The simple fact was that they saw that we had the **will** to go out there and do it. Others may have analysed the task and then shelved the plan. Especially a plan drawn up on the back of a few sheets of A4 paper, typed up on an Amstrad CPC 464 and printed out on an old dot matrix, right? But for us it worked.

This is the first lesson. Selling a business takes many steps and can be more difficult than you first anticipate. As long as you understand this everything will come through in the end. One thing I have experienced is that there is **always** a buyer for the right business at the right price. Finding them is the key.

3. The key

Here's another flashback, do bear with me:

When I was about fourteen, I was standing in line with a bunch of boys and girls at a dojo (where martial arts are practised and taught). I was there because, coming home one night from school, I had been beaten up by a couple of boys who had mistaken me for someone else in a school gang fight. I went home with my shirt bloodied, knowing that I had to find a way to protect myself. I found a karate class and joined the next day.

Now, a few years on, we were in the line-up for a specific reason, to **kick** apart a thick piece of wood that my Sensei (a fifth degree black-belt) was holding in his hands. None of us had done anything like it before and everyone was scared, to say the least. The first boy stood in a special form (stance) and kicked the wood with all his might. We heard a harsh bang and watched him limp back. He was considerably larger than me. A girl was called up next, she was a high degree belt holder, known for her polished technique, and she too was quite strong. She made two attempts before she was carried away!

Then I was called up. Seeing the other two on the floor made me gulp but I did not have much choice, I had joined this class of my own free **will**.

As I took up the stance, I **knew** there was **no way** I was going to break that wood. The previous kicks had not even scratched or dented it. Sensei gave me the look and said 'Haa', which means 'Do it' in a dojo. As I gave it my all I thought I heard my little toe crack as pain rocketed through my body – and that piece of wood was still there smirking back at me. After one more try, it was nearly time for me to join my comrades on the floor but my teacher, who must have seen something in me, told me to stay.

What came next was a revelation that I have used countless times in difficult situations to achieve my goals. For this I am thankful to my Sensei.

He said, standing with his hands outstretched, holding the indestructible piece of wood in front of him, 'Hold on there a minute. Now I want you not to kick the wood but to kick me. I want you to aim for my stomach not the wood.'

To kick his stomach meant that I would have to aim through the wood.

'You **can** do it,' he said, 'just think as if the wood is not there.'

The dojo went silent, I felt everyone looking at me and I swear it felt like a slow motion film scene. There was no loud bang, no pain, but when I looked up, there I was standing with two broken pieces of wood on the floor and the entire dojo clapping. This was the first time in our year that anyone had broken wood. This was usually only taught to blackbelts and we were juniors. Had I delivered the kick? Yes, but there was one big change that I believe was the **key**.

There was no bang and no pain, in fact the pain from my previous kick had also gone. I had figured out the greatest lesson of all. I had done it with nothing more than the **will** and belief that the wood could be broken. In that nanosecond when my teacher said to me 'You can do it', I believed him so absolutely that I was going to do it, that I did it. The result was undeniable.

I did not think about it philosophically until many years later. At that age I just enjoyed the fame that came from being known as 'The One'. Yes that felt good. However, a lot happened in those few seconds before and after the kick that I will refer to later on.

4. Can do, will do

There is something so simple and basic that we all get wrong. To do anything you must first have made up your mind to do it, then find the ability to do it and, most importantly, follow through.

If you have decided to sell your business, do it! Many business sales are held back because the buyer finds that the seller is not keen. Alternatively, sellers may find that buyers are time wasters or crafty thinkers. Sometimes an enquirer is not genuinely interested in buying but is looking for something new as they have nothing better to do that day. I have dedicated the whole of Chapter 5 to recognising and differentiating between buyers.

Essentially, you are not going to sell your business quickly, effectively or for the right price just by placing an advert in the paper or online, or even by engaging a business broker, if you are not in the right mindset. First, it is critical that you are sure this is the action you want to take, then that you have the ability to do it and finally that you follow through.

5. To sell or not to sell, that is the question

If you are unsure what to do, seek expert advice. Look closely at the initial reason you had for selling. Is it still justified or have there been material changes in your circumstances?

Were you selling because business was slow or fading? Was it old age? Identify what is making you unsure. You will find it is the un**will**ingness that will stop you from getting the right buyer quickly. It will be the same things that will hinder you from getting the asking price when you do find a buyer.

I have come across many instances when selling has not been the right choice. The owner of a printing factory in West London told me he wanted out. He had been printing leaflets for a long time with the help of a business partner who was now moving abroad. Profits were not enough to keep going. His business partner was of the same opinion and wanted to sell. However, my friend was unsure so I asked him to seek a better option. He ended up buying his partner's share of the business, acquiring better machines and trebling his takings. He made the right choice by not selling. The business today is worth three times what it was worth when he was thinking of selling.

I was once told that businesses only sell when they are ready, not when you are ready. I believe if you are ready in your mind to sell, that really is all it takes. For instance, in one business sale I was involved in, the client was so focused on selling, he did not care what he was going to get for it. Even if it meant getting less than what he had invested. It was a factory selling fuel oils made from waste oil; sourcing the raw oil was a nightmare; there had been all sorts of problems setting up the factory in the first place. He just wanted out. When he contacted me, I knew immediately that his business would sell, but I also knew it would sell at a good price. In the end it sold even in the most economic turbulent time.

If you are of the mind that you want to sell your business – or even establish a business to sell – then you **will** succeed. The discoveries I have made along the way will help you achieve this goal quickly.

Chapter 2: The Virtual World

1. Preparation is everything

Now let's get started with the easier, but important, stuff – the preparation stage. Once this is done the rest (the sale process and what to do after) will all come together, believe me.

Remember the karate kick? Let me tell you a little bit more about what happened that day.

When my Sensei said he wanted me to go for his stomach instead of the wood, I involuntarily did a number of things that I did not appreciate until later. Small things which will allow **anyone** to break large pieces of wood **with ease**.

For one, I moved closer to the wood so that my kick would reach my target – the Sensei's stomach – a good few inches behind the board.

Next, I was no longer thinking about hitting the board. I had not forgotten about breaking the wood, but it did take my mind off the pain associated with the act. The failure of those before me had 'taught me' that I could not do it. After all, one of the boys was bigger than me. Do not let other people's mistakes or actions influence your mindset about what you can and cannot do. They may be reacting to their own experience of life, which may be very different to yours. By all means listen to them, but make up your own mind.

Because my fear of pain had been temporarily dulled my breathing slowed and, when I did break the wood, I exhaled with a loud shout. If you exercise regularly or go to the gym, you'll know how important breathing can be. Take too many breaths during a routine and that alone can tire you out, or even make you lose consciousness; take too few and you soon become exhausted.

Another instinctive manoeuvre was that, before lifting my leg to kick, I had to bring my knee much higher up than during my previous kick, which again increased my reach.

Finally, my eyes were not looking at the wood, but through it.

So, what does all this mean to someone selling a business? The secret is all in the preparation.

It is what you put into the **before** that will determine how easily and quickly you will follow through. It is all the small manoeuvres that will make the difference; the preparation that **will** increase your **will** to sell at your asking price.

Let me show you how this can be done.

2. Building a website

Websites are an essential tool if you are selling your business. In today's world the internet has become, the research tool for everything. From buying the right choice of toothbrush to finding your life partner, the internet does seem to offer it all. Anyone buying your business will research it online. Google is today's preferred search engine and, in the world of website optimisation, 85% of the searches carried out in Britain are done through Google. Your website does not have to rank highly on the search engine since, if your buyer has spoken to you, he will have seen it. However, if you have no website, what can your prospective buyer do to research the business?

2.1. It needs to be visually pleasing

A website that looks really dull, built without the user in mind, is not going to work. Conversely, a too colourful website may also send the wrong message. As an example, if you are selling business reports or digital data, a clown dancing in the background will not work for you. However, if you are selling children's toys it might work well.

What does a website cost nowadays? The usual answer is how long is a piece of string? In my opinion that is wrong. I have been able to use template designs very effectively. You can purchase a flash website for very little, which in most cases will halve your costs in producing a stunning website. Type *website template* into Google and you will come across some good templates for your line of business that are ready to use.

Some template selling websites offer to remove your chosen template from their store for an outright price, so you are the only one with that look. Really? No, of course not, someone may have purchased that template before you, so don't bother going for that option. Most templates are sold by third party companies so there is no real copyright unless that particular one has never been sold before.

2.2. Content is important

There is no point in a good-looking website if the information on it is misleading, wrong or contains nothing of relevance. The top portion of your website, which most browsers show without scrolling, needs to say (in the shortest of phrases) what your business does. Do not use clichés or clever word manipulation. This is important, as you will see in the next section. The easiest way of obtaining content is to scroll through the websites of similar companies and see what they say. A costly, but more expert way, is to hire a content writer. There are many services out there, most charge a few pence per word. Each website should have at least 5 to 10 pages, each page having about 250–300 words.

Here is an average breakdown of costs to get a good website:

Website template and customisation: £150

Copywriter to write the content: £150

Image purchases: £50

You saying you did the lot: Priceless.

2.3. Website optimisation

Many buyers will research your website by Googling relevant keywords and seeing how it fares. It is difficult for someone to find your website amongst the billions of websites out there. Even those that know you, will still just type the main words into a search engine and click on the first non-sponsored link. Your website designer should be able to provide you with some input to optimise your homepage. It is technical stuff but, in a nutshell, the website address (the domain name or part after the www.), the way the website is described in the coding description, and the meta keywords all play a big role in how a search engine's spider (The software that sees your site) finds your site. This is why content is so important.

As an example, a website selling toys, with content describing books and with a web address that contains nothing about books or toys, is going to be lost in internet space. There is free software and useful tools, such as Google Analytics, that can help you. The more you research this and utilize, the more your site will be optimised.

This all helps when your prospective buyer searches the internet to find out who your competitors are. If your website is not found in their searches then it may lead them to think that, if they could not find you, how would their customers find them if they bought your business. Always put yourself in your prospective buyer's shoes and ask how you would rate yourself.

2.4. Contact Us page

Finally, the website must have a good, clear Contact Us page. It should list your office numbers, and email addresses you use for business. Beware of software crawling through websites searching for contact details, which are then sold to database companies. If you put your information in a picture format rather than as text then spam finders and email/phone catching software will not find it.

The Contact Us page could be a simple form that people fill in so that the information is sent to you by email.

3. Image

Whatever you do, your business should have a brand. The brand name says so much about you. It is like the number plate on a car.

When purchasing a used car, the first thing everyone looks at is the car registration. Firstly, this identifies the car as the one being sold. Secondly, but subconsciously, you also look at the condition of the plate. While everyone looks at the overall condition of the car, private sellers usually forget how important it is to have a good, clean number plate. It has probably been on the car since it was first registered and so it tells the 'inside story'. A damaged number plate, or one with faded letters, tells how the car has been maintained. Right ? Wrong. Look at the plates on used cars outside showrooms. You will not find one that is damaged, faded or even dirty. They know its importance and will buy a new plate for an old car. The car will sell faster and better than if it was being sold with the old plate. It is so simple and important, yet many of us do not realise it.

The image, or logo, you give your business has to be right. The logo has to give a clear indication of your service or product. Many logos have been designed very cleverly: like the Fedex logo, with its subliminal arrow in the white space; Coca-Cola's distinctive shape that echoes a flowing drink. Image puts you out there.

Many logos also have a short catchline that says a little about their service or product. An example is the McDonalds golden arches followed by the phrase 'i'm lovin' it'.

You only need to go to any high street to see more examples. All these are image 'hooks', in memory books they are sometimes referred to as 'handles' and place a significant message in the minds of the customers. In our case, this is what you want your prospective buyer to remember about your business. If you do not have a logo or brand for your company, your business has no place in space! Just a company name is no good. Put pen to paper and start drawing. Better still, hire a professional designer to do it. Logo designers charge anywhere from £50 to £250 depending on how deeply they have to research to get the right image for you.

4. The video

There is a very effective tool that can improve both your image and the quality of your business, whatever stage it is at. That is, make a video about it.

In my experience there is nothing that sells a business like a video about what you do. Why is a video so important? For one thing, placing a video on your website greatly increases its ranking on Google. For another, in the real world today people will not give you more than 90 seconds to introduce yourself. In fact, most will be bored by the time you've even spoken your first few words of introduction because they will have heard the same openings many times over. Why is a video different? Simply put, if you can make it interesting you will have captured the viewer's attention. The mind does not need to read words, it is watching images and animation as your message is both seen and heard.

Why did we like cartoons when we were small? The simplicity of animation told us to trust what we saw. This is why your video should be an animation instead of real footage. You are giving your viewer a short break from reality. This is pleasing and relaxing. What you are doing is presenting your ideas without thrusting a CV at them. We've all heard that a picture speaks a thousand words; a video can speak a million!

One of the greatest advantages of the video is that it is by far the quickest way for someone to understand what your business does. There is an exact science behind how long your video should be, what it must contain and how it is put together. It should be exactly 90 seconds long. Any more and you bore your viewer, any less and you might not get across your full message. So what should the video contain?

4.1. The script

The script is **the** most important part of the video. For a 90-second video, at a normal reading speed and allowing for pauses, there should be approximately 220–250 words in the script.

Ideally, you know your business. The script should focus on showing a quality business with quality products and services. Start by dividing the words into the sections you need to portray your business. Begin with a quick introduction, displaying your logos and branding. Do not condescend to your viewer by going on about the logo, why you are such a good business person or what your business started from. The introduction should be no longer than 50 words.

Winston Churchill was once asked to give a speech. He said, 'If you want me to give 5 minutes it will take me a week to get ready. If you want 30 minutes, I will need 3 days. If you want an hour, I am ready now.'

Be concise and clear. We are not all a 21st century Charles Dickens, but if you cannot write a concise description of your business get in an expert.

The next 100 or so words should talk about the business, the quality of the products and services. The final 20–30 words **must** convey the next action the viewer needs to take in order to find out more. This is usually done by reference to your website or contact details. One way is to use Quick Request (QR) codes; these are codes that can be scanned by smart phone cameras and translate the image into a website or contact details. With so many smart phones in use displaying a QR code on the final animation screen of the video can work wonders, just make sure you give the right information. They look something like this:

When you scan this QR code it will generate a message about this book. Give it a go.

While writing the script, remember your important goal: **you want to sell the business.** However, do **not** make this the main message in your video, unless you are making several then one can be dedicated to the 'sell'. I'll discuss what the 'sell' entails in the following chapters.

4.2. Storyboarding

Storyboarding is the way the words in the script are organised into still images to show how the video will progress. I help the storyboarder by writing out what I want to happen in the video in each part of the script.

4.3. Voiceover

A voiceover is the audio part of the video. A voiceover artist is someone who knows how best to use their voice for the script. The storyboard and script help the voiceover artist to say the words in a way that translates properly for the video. In some places they may need to add more emphasis and in others more character. All important elements of the video.

The human voice engages the key sense of hearing while the animation engages the eyes. The recording has to be done professionally or it sounds amateurish and you stand to lose quality. There is no preference to using either a male or a female voice, it depends on the business. For example, if your business sold feminine products, it may be better to use a female voice.

The cost of hiring a studio and engaging a voiceover artist can run into hundreds, even thousands, of pounds. In most cases you will need at least two recordings. Even if you have that kind of money there is no guarantee you will get a good recording. The question is, how do you find a professional voiceover artist who will work for a reasonable price?

I have found that there is a lot of talent that wants to gain recognition. You can find some on talent websites such as **www.starnow.co.uk**, where you can post ads. You will find BBC-style speakers as well as amateurs, make your selection carefully. Many of these people will already have an association with a recording studio or have professional recording equipment at home. Ask them to record the audio themselves and send it to you in an appropriate form such as an .mp3 file. One advert on StarNow can leave you spoilt for choice. Get at least two recordings, one at normal speed and one at a slightly slower pace.

4.4. Animation

This is the part that only an expert can do. Special effects are expensive and you really need to know where to find the right animator. The question I always get asked is that how much is this going to cost? A small 30-second animation can cost as much as £3000, so is this where the idea stops? No way!

As I said, talent is everywhere and you can give it the chance to gain recognition for a small fee, while getting the work you want. It usually takes an animator about 2 to 3 weeks to get everything ready for you to finalise.

The animator has to take the script and storyboard, use the voiceover and combine everything into a video. The most used software for this is Adobe After Effects, which is good if you know how to work it, but most of us should let an expert do it. Making a video is a labour intensive job and there are little shortcuts that can be taken. Experts also have access to the source files that are needed.

There are outsourcing websites where you can place an advert and people compete to bid for your work. The best platforms I have found are **www.elance.com** and **www.peopleperhour.com**. Ideally you will spend anything from US$250 to make your animation; since these talented individuals are located in far-flung places, such as India and China, it is a good local rate. Spend more and you will get a better animator.

Most of these sites require you to deposit the money in a holding account called an *escrow account*. This means the funds are not released to the worker until they complete the job, however, as the money is in escrow, they have confirmation that you have the funds to complete the job. These freelancers are very competitive and they like good feedback, so they will work to please and do little extras to help them get a better feedback rating. Animators with a higher feedback rating will usually demand higher payment.

The size of your video can be changed, but it is usually a good idea to tell the animator if you intend to upload your video to a website such as YouTube. They will then design it to a size which is suitable. Ask the animator to supply your file in either .flv or .mpg/.mp4 formats, which can be directly placed on these video sharing sites.

4.5. Final cut

Once the video is made, you will be given a video that needs to be edited to give your cut (sometimes referred to as the final cut). Look at the whole video and iron out any potential problems.

Since these animators are working in different countries their first language may not be English so check any spellings if there are any words in the animation. I once received a video that was brilliant in terms of its animation, but it was bogged down with spelling mistakes.

Check with the animator where the images come from. They do not always know what copyright is, and may have copied them from other websites. One animator I used copied an image directly from our supplier's site. I had to ask him to change it immediately.

Finally, ask the animator to send you all the source files. These are the working files used to create the video. It will usually consist of one or two Adobe After Effect or software files and several files with images and small partial videos. They can take up to one gigabyte of memory space, which is too large to send via email. Use a third party transfer service. I use yousendit.com as it is free.

Making the video can be fun and the results sometimes very satisfying. So, now you have made the video, what do you do with it?

5. Marketing your website and video

5.1. The website

There are several ways of marketing your website referred to as Search Engine Optimisation, or SEO for short. There are ways to change the coding in the source files of your main landing page so that search engines can recognise them. In general, the website coding has parts which refer to the main heading, the description and keywords in relation to its content. If similar words are found in each category then the website is somewhat optimised. For instance, a website selling flowers called flowers.com, which has the description of 'We sell flowers and are florists', with the keywords 'flowers', will rank high in search engines. However, even using all these elements won't guarantee a top placement.

5.2. The video

Get your video on all the video sites there are. There are about ten of which the best are YouTube, Dailymotion and Metacafe are amongst the top three. There are several tweaks you can make on each site that optimises your video further. These include: adding a caption, a description; and in some instances you can also add the location of the business. Do as much as you can.

6. Social media

Social media, such as Facebook and Twitter, are common places for you to advertise your services. Open an account with them in your company name and drop in a description and pictures with links to your website and video. It's all free.

Facebook has a business section called Pages. This allows you to create dedicated pages about your website, or pages that specialise in niche products. Creating the right profile page is important. Remember that a lot of what is on Facebook is optimised by them and appears on search engines such as Google. So get it right. Upload your logo. Good descriptions about your company and images with tags will help. You can also upload your video to your Facebook page. Remember it is all about impressions and getting found.

Twitter on the other hand, is more about getting to know others. Twitter also offer advertising where you can gain followers. Getting the right type of followers is essential. They have many videos that can help you set up your account on twitter.

LinkedIn is more of a membership site that allows you to link to other businessmen and businesswomen. You can pass messages to each other and also recommend each other. At the time of signing up they offer two types of accounts, one is free, the other is a premium account. Go with the free account then upgrade when you feel the benefits of the premium account are for you.

There are many social media sites and not all will be good for your business. Remember, when you sell all these will go to the new owner, enhancing the perceived value of your business.

It is a good idea to keep all your usernames and passwords different for each site, since they are prone to cyber attack.

This is how your business needs to exist in the virtual world. How you prepare for the real world comes next.

Chapter 3: The Real World

1. Preparing the business plan

Every business needs a business plan, especially if you are going to sell it. A business plan gives you a 40% higher chance of selling. Why? Because the new owner can grasp everything about the business in just a few pages.

So, what is a business plan?

Basically, it identifies what the business does, who runs it, how it is run, its SWOT (Strengths, Weakness, Opportunities and Threats) and a summary of accounts.

Below are the main headings for a business plan with a brief summary of what they should contain:

Executive Summary

> A summary of what the business is and does, should be no longer than one page
> A brief description of products, services and customers

Contents

> The contents of the document with page numbers

Introduction

> Why you have produced this business plan; if it is to sell the business, say so
> Prospective buyers may use it to get loans or credit to buy the business

The Opportunity

> The business concept
> Service description

Company Description

> Give the full registration numbers, VAT numbers and all the business identifiers (including the address)
> Vision: what the business hopes to achieve in the long run

Mission statement: what the business is, or hopes to achieve, in the immediate future

Industry Analysis

Describe the overall market for the business
List the raw materials
Outline the demand for the product
Comment on the competition
Present the key performance indicators; safety and costings

Target Market

Target customers
Areas of operation
Revenue streams
Competitive edge

Strategy

Strategic analysis of the overall market
Marketing strategy specific to the business
Strategic partnerships

Operations

Facilities and offices
Hours of operation
Systems and controls
Risk evaluation
Development plan

Management and Organisation

Key employees and principals and their salaries
Consultants and professional resources

Long Term Development and Exit Plan

Exit strategy (the sale)

Financial Summary (must contain all the following points)

Start-up cost
Capital expenditure
STEEPLE analysis: social, technological, economical, environmental, political, legal and ethical influences on the business

> SWOT analysis: usually displayed in a diagram illustrating the strengths, weaknesses, opportunities and threats to the business
> Risk analysis
> Profit and loss statement
> Cash flow
> Annual profit and loss statements
> Balance sheets.

The sections dealing with accounts can be done by your accountant. However, as the owner and seller, you must have a summary of the above in your head. This will come in handy when you draw up the business for sale advert. The most important figures are the turnover, gross and net profits of the business.

You may already have a business plan, but to sell the business you may need to revise it.

If, on the other hand, the list sounds like a foreign language then you need to get an expert in to create the plan. I have found people who can compile this document for less than you might think using Elance.com.

You can do it yourself if you **believe** in your business methods and are familiar with the above.

2. The marketing plan

Your marketing plan should tie up with the business plan and there is a lot of common ground between the marketing and business plans so you can incorporate the two. However, there is one key difference. The marketing plan looks at the business from the outside as opposed to the business plan's more internal viewpoint.

3. The accounts

The last section of the business plan is the accounts. It may be an advantage to keep the accounts separate from the business plan. For instance, a prospective buyer may only want to see the accounts; internal management buyouts or purchasers with a similar business won't want a long narrative about the business.

Remember, accounts are about figures, but you'd be surprised at the number of people who get their numbers wrong. Do your accounts in a spread sheet that includes the facility to check sums. Even better, use an accountant with specialist software.

The last thing you want is a buyer pointing out silly mistakes in the calculations.

4. The business ledgers

I know all this talk of paperwork sounds boring, but someone's got to do it. The next step is to make sure your supplier and sales ledgers exist and are accessible. You'd think a business would have these in order, but I am surprised at the number of people who don't even bother to keep them because:

'We know who our suppliers are, we talk to them everyday.'

'My customers know me.'

That is all very well, but your prospective buyer doesn't, so make sure it is all written down.

If you have 'walk in' customers then obviously they may not all be known to you, but you do need to know how many of them there are. if you run an online store, how many unique customers do you get per week or per month?

Records are so easy to keep, but also so easy to forget to keep.

5. The business

When was the last time you checked up on the day-to-day running of the business to see if it is OK? It might be a good idea, unless you are contemplating an asset-only sale.

Even in an asset-only sale, where you are only selling the hardware and not the goodwill, the business plan and all the 'virtual' elements are still very important. They enable prospective buyers to make a correct assessment about the business but, more importantly, they **add value.**

Make sure any loose ends with your customers are tidied up and avoid entering into any new supplier arrangements. Sometimes new suppliers prove problematic and existing ones may not treat you with the same level of respect if they realise that your loyalty is now split. This may spell disaster if prospective buyers ask for your trading history from a supplier only find that you have been with them for a short time.

As for any disgruntled employees, now might be a good time to make amends, or redundancies. Nothing spells disaster more than an employee bad-mouthing you or your business. Employees can be your greatest asset so don't make light decisions about key ones; if their contribution to the prospects of the business is high they can increase its worth.

6. Dust away

It is really important to **keep the business premises clean and tidy**. Whatever the state of your business this at least indicates potential.

Keep your desk tidy. An untidy desk means an untidy business work ethic. This applies all the way through the company.

My father used to work for BP Shell in Africa, his boss would wipe his fingers across all his managers' desks to see the amount of dust. My father soon rose to the top simply because his working attitude and ethics was seen reflected in the cleanliness of his workspace. He later went on to run his own construction company and become a ship owner. Tidiness goes a long way.

Make sure the filed ledgers and the files on the business computers are organised in such a way that information can be retrieved easily. Delete any unnecessary data but back up everything. Computers have a nasty way of playing up at crucial times. At the very least, you will gain the respect of any potential buyer.

Chapter 4: Ready For The Sale

So now you have the virtual and real worlds covered and the paperwork ready. Time to get ready for the sale and the advertising.

1. Look at other businesses for sale

The best way to get a feel for the way you need to word your advert is to look at similar ones. Search in the relevant sections online and in the papers for adverts containing the key words that match your business. Look at the adverts as if you were a potential buyer: what catches your eye; where did you find them; which site ranked highest in your online searches?

Remember, Google now looks at your physical location whenever you do a search so that a similar search in a different location may yield different results. For this reason try several searches and look at the same adverts over a couple of days to see how they are doing. I do not condone the following but, if you want to get a better idea about a similar business, send an enquiry to the seller. The price they quote may give you some indication as to how you should price your business.

2. The advert

Where you place your advert does matter but you need a professional looking one to start with. So let us get to work on that.

2.1. The heading

The advert needs to sound personal, as though a human is placing it, not a machine. The heading is ***the most*** important part of the advert, it is what will be seen first. Produce a bad one and you will lose your perfect buyer.

Take a look at these examples of good and bad headings:

Bad	Good
Printing business for sale	Profitable print business for sale
Business going out of business, please get us out!	Quick sale, owner retiring from current business
Suppliers not giving us credit, customers not paying money, anyone interested?	Fresh business looking for new buyer with contacts to boost business. Very low price

OK, some are a tiny bit exaggerated. Nevertheless, headings should be kept short and simple, some advertisers allow you to place a subheading, or short text, after the main heading. In this case, the main heading should be no longer than five or six words then elaborate in the subheading. Remember, in most online adverts it is only the words in the main heading that are searchable.

2.2. The main body of the text

According to research by Forbes, the average adult's attention span is 8 seconds and most will stop listening after 5 seconds. Unless you hook them you lose them and they move on. Telling someone what your business does in this amount of time is a talent and needs to be researched properly. Do not depend on your improvisational skills in order to get the right message across.

Your main body of text needs to be as much to the point as the heading. Remember, after the first 8 seconds you are on to the next 8 seconds. So, before committing words to paper, ask yourself these questions (with thanks to Forbes 'best pitch'):

1. What problem does your business solve?

Customers always buy painkillers, not vitamins.

Where to Start: Complete the sentence, 'My company helps _____ who are _____.' or 'Customers rely on my company because we are the best at _____.'

2. What are your business' voice and values?

Are they communicated consistently in everything?

Where to Start: Ask customers to name positive and negative adjectives that best describe your business. Use these to gain an extra mile in the wording, mentioning only the positives. See below for more on this.

3. Who is your community? What type of customers are attracted to what your business sells?

Where to Start: Look at your current clients. What is the profile you now serve? (Additionally, is this the community of customers you want to be serving?)

OK. I am ready to listen. You have my undivided attention for the next 8 seconds. Go.

Remember let it flow. Don't be too obsessed with 'selling'. This is a classic mistake.

Speak about the business strengths, **not** about any negative points, however small or relevant to a buyer. Your buyer may be one of the 'tigers' out there ready to spring onto a good opportunity and you just turned your business into a sheep with a small remark about a business weakness. Here is a classic example:

> Print business for sale
>
> Our printing business is for sale. We are located on the high street and service the local community for print jobs. _Yes, there is a lot of competition from online and other shops nearby,_ but we pride ourselves on our customers' loyalty…

At this point you have lost the buyer. Remember, your target is to attract a potential purchaser. The fact that you decided to mention details from the business plan can put a keen buyer off. He is probably already speaking to another business for sale, even though they may have more competition than you. The truth is that every business has competition but you need to help your reader picture themselves buying into yours.

Whilst honesty is the best policy, it is better to let your buyer discover or inform them of any weaknesses or flaws later on when there is further interest. That is not the advert's job, which is the **first** thing a buyer sees. Even a little error here will cost you the buyer. Do it right and don't lose the war before the battle has even begun.

However, if there is a major issue – such as the business is not yours or it is being liquidated – then do not conceal these facts. Beware of using brokers who advertise businesses for sale but who don't actually inform the enquirer that they are brokers.

Now let us look how the above advert should have been worded:

> Highly profitable print business for sale
>
> Printing is one of the most highly sought after businesses. Our company services the local community's print requirements. Having built up a large database of loyal repeat customers, both commercial and trade, we flourish in the heart of London...

Keep facts simple and do not delve into talking about specifics unless they really matter. Remember, it's all about keeping the reader interested and hooked. By the end they should be desperate to send you an enquiry!

Ideally the main body should be about 250 words long; don't repeat facts; don't go too deeply into figures but do mention these four key things:

1. Turnover
2. Gross profit
3. Net profit
4. Selling price

If the business has not traded sufficiently to generate pleasing figures, or is a startup, then you will also need to mention:

5. Projected turnover
6. Projected gross profit
7. Projected net profit.

These are the figures that ideally determine the level of interest you will get, so **get them right**. The number of adverts in which people neglect these essentials is astounding. Some do not even know them, but every serious enquirer will expect you to know these figures by heart.

I have been to so many sales pitches where the seller answers my enquiries with : 'I'll have to ask my accountant, he will send them over to you'. I've usually lost interest before I reach home.

If you, as the business owner, do not know these basic facts, you are either concealing them or cannot be running a good business. Either way, you have lost credibility if the only person who knows your figures is someone else.

Everyone wants to know why a business is for sale so that they can determine if there is a functioning business or whether the owner is leaving a sinking ship. If you are going to mention the reason for the sale in the advert then be honest.

2.3. The end part

Congratulations, you have made the reader come to the end of the advert. Now you must mention what they have to do next and what they can expect in return. End with your contact details, ideally both a landline and a mobile number. Highlight a number where they can leave a message or be directly connected. An email address is also an advantage.

2.4. The other parts

You produced a video for a very good reason and now is the time to use it. A video is the clearest, simplest and most concise way to show your potential buyer what your business is all about. Even if you are advertising in print you need to include links to your uploaded video. This can be either your own website or another third party website where your video is showcased.

Placing an advert for your business sale is very much like placing your friend's profile on a marriage or dating site. If you really want them to get noticed you need to upload their picture. You need to make sure your friend sounds attractive both physically and as a personality. Imagine the physical part as our 'real world' and the personality as the 'virtual world'. Both are important to get your friend a 'date' or as in the case of your business an 'enquirer'.

An advert without a picture will look dull and is less likely to be looked at. Although, if an advert cannot accommodate a picture or video, try different ways to get noticed. The first business I ever sold was advertised in LOOT. This was not an ideal place to advertise, but within weeks I had a few enquiries. No picture, no video, but what I did do was make sure the wording was eye-catching. I also placed the advert inside a thick, bold box that made it stand out from the page. Open any magazine with a classified section and see where your eyes go to first and where you actually start to read. It will be the boxed and underlined adverts. Do not USE CAPITALS since it looks like you are shouting at someone – sorry didn't mean to shout there.

Getting noticed is important. The good part is that not everyone is going to be trying. Believe it or not, some people are scared of advertising. They believe that people will come to them. Why advertise? Who wants to speak to strangers anyway? That has been a 'no-no' since childhood.

Let your competitors worry like that. You advertise your heart out! The more exposure you have the better the responses you will get. So, where to advertise?

3. The right places to advertise

Let's look at the example of your friend on a dating site. Will you place them in the free section along with another 1000 adverts? Or will you put them in the best possible place?

You want to give your friend the best chance of finding a good mate, not a freeloader. Placing a free advert is telling the reader something about the advertiser, so beware. You do not want to portray the wrong image after all your hard work. You may get lucky, but your chances are slim.

You need to place your advert where you want it to be found. By not thinking too carefully and looking only at the cost of placing the advert, all your hard work may go to waste. Advertising an expensive business in the classified one-liners is not going to work. To attract the right crowd advertise where they are looking.

After several business and franchise sales, I have found some places where placing an advert will get you good results:

www.businessesforsale.com A website that specialises in what it says. They are also highly web optimised so your title (e.g. café, guesthouse or factory) will come up in Google searches. They charge according to the number of months you advertise with them.

Daltonsbusiness.com Web edition of their once-published magazine, this website will generate a decent number of enquires.

Business-sale.com Another website that charges a flat fee for advertising. However, your asking price has to be above £150k and your turnover above £300k. Otherwise advertise on their sister website: **www.bizsale.co.uk**

Advertise on one first and then another. There are other avenues, and I don't discourage the use of any of them, but do check their ranking or circulation to make sure your money is spent well. Don't splash out on every website or journal. Target ones specific to your industry or those that have a good 'foot tread'.

Many people advertise that their business is for sale on their website. This is not always a good sign and could scare away their regular customers.

4. Word of mouth

This last method is getting the word around your social circles. You may know a cousin who has just sold his business, or maybe a friend or relative has been made redundant and they need something to do. There is nothing wrong in being an opportunist when it comes to getting your business sold. You may open a door for someone who really needs it.

Chapter 5: Buyers

1.   Buyers come in all shapes and sizes

You need to find the right buyer for your business and stay away from the sharks and false enquirers who are everywhere. It is essential to identify and keep away the time wasters.

Let us look at five types of buyer.

1.1. The sharks

These are the most dangerous and you need to identify them quickly. They will appear to be the most interested in your business. But what do sharks do? They have a keen interest in their food and will eat you alive, smashing your objectives and creating real havoc. Why do they do this? Because their key objective is to get money out of you one way or another: they want your account details so they can 'transfer a million pounds'; they will offer your buying price, or even appear to negotiate a price, before they have even asked you about your business. They may know a lot about the business, but what cannot be researched today on the internet? Essentially they are **scammers**.

They can pose as buyers from anywhere in the world and appear to have local, UK-based contacts that will give you a UK mobile number to call. However, when you ask about them they tend to be elusive and give long-winded descriptions about nothing important. They will appear to be completely and truly 'in love' with your business but, believe me, they are totally in love with your money and they will try to get it off you.

I was once approached by such a shark and, not realising it at the time, I responded to his enquiry. From the beginning he could only sing the praises of the fantastic opportunity I was offering and how thankful he was to me for selling my business. I was a bit wary since he had not really asked me the commonest questions about the print franchise business I was selling, not even the terms or the reason for the sale. This should have rung alarm bells instantly.

Later on, he said that he had some problems in transferring the monies from his home country because the local bank manager had to be 'paid' to make the transfer and he needed that amount from me. By this time I had already decided that I had heard enough. With age comes wisdom and I always find it reassuring to ask my father about any such matters. Luckily, my father was of the same mind and advised me not to pursue the matter further. I stopped corresponding with the shark buyer, despite his repeated calls and him even saying at one stage that he had 'negotiated' a better rate for me.

Beware of the intelligent scammers. They are after your account details, your signature and anything else that can be used. Don't give your personal information to anyone unless you can verify who they are. Because sellers can feel that the onus is on them to prove their business worth, scammers take advantage of this vulnerable thinking and boost your self-confidence so you believe in them. Don't fall for it. Listen to people who say it as it is, not the way you want to hear it.

I have heard of several variations on the above scam, even to where the deal is brought to such a stage that you are even paid. However, your account is then suddenly frozen because it was used as a transfer medium for someone else who has been scammed. Be very wary if the buyer is only interested in a specific purchase figure, especially if it is more than your asking price. This is effectively a scam on someone else and you are being used as a 'money mule'. It is usually some time before the scam is revealed as the other party is waiting for goods or services, by then the scammers may have moved your machinery and stock to another location.

1.2. The competitors

These are false enquirers. Ideally, they are checking the market for what you are selling so as to gauge a selling price for their own business. We may have even used this tactic ourselves. They are not always bad buyers if they are after buying out the competition. However, such cases are rare since people in the same line of trade seldom buy a business exactly alike.

In more sinister cases they may be after your trade secrets, such as who your suppliers or buyers are. The way to get around this is to word your NDA (Non-Disclosure Agreement) in such a manner that any information or trader names supplied cannot be contacted by the enquirer for a minimum of one year. This will filter out these false buyers.

1.3. The viewers

These are the number of times your advert has been viewed. Some websites allow you to see how many 'views' or 'impressions' your advert has received. It is a good way to monitor the interest. Your advert will most definitely be viewed more times than the number of enquiries you get. This is because many people will view your advert and then decide it is not for them. This is quite normal. However, if you find that you are getting fewer enquiries than 5% of the total number of views then there maybe something in your advert that is putting people off. Get someone else to read it if you cannot find the problem.

Perhaps your advert is in the wrong section; perhaps people are being misled by the heading. Check all the possibilities. Unless your business is selling ten pound notes for five pounds, you will get enquiries.

Remember, somewhere amongst your viewers is your perfect buyer.

1.4. The dreamers

These are simply delusional people who wish they could own your business. Most of the time they don't have the money or even the expertise to run the business. However, they are good dreamers. In my experience they are not all to be discounted. After all, everyone is allowed to dream. They can be identified easily. For one, they will imagine your business in a different place, not in its current position or trading with your present customer base. Most likely, they will ask few questions and the ones they do ask might seem odd. They always seem to talk about the future and you will be able to sense this in their body language. Not all dreamers are time-wasters, so give them some time. One sure way to find a dreamer is to check whether they have all the finance in place or whether they would be interested in seller finance. This is where the seller provides the buyer with either a part-payment, or a complete instalment structure. They will grab at the chance and then the conversation will move on to how the money can be raised and how much you might give them as capital trade cash. The business itself will disappear as a topic altogether.

Some dreamers have the ability to follow through on their dreams, so be prepared, you might be looking at your ideal buyer. If you offer an 'earn-out', where you let them pay you out of the sales of goods and services, you will need a good lawyer to word the sale agreement. Keep securities and charges over all the business assets.

1.5. The employee

People under the employee banner do not speak the language of the businessman and are usually individuals who are actually looking for employment. They are not deceptive, which is a good thing. Some may even offer to share the hours of work. If they offer you a partnership in your own business we class them as dreamers (see 'earn-out' above).

Many businesses have been sold to management so it may be a good idea to keep them on the back burner if you are willing to let someone else run your business for a share.

Ask all the questions that you would if they had come to you for actual employment and ask all the relevant questions about their history and credentials. Check on and phone up references.

Draw up a contract that does not last longer than six months. Then, if either party does not want to continue after that there should be no hard feelings.

Remember you are now in it for the long haul.

2. Recognising your buyer

Here are the indicators that you have a serious enquirer:

2.1. The timer

There is one thing that is common to **all** the serious buyers I have ever had, time. If you have given them a time to meet you, they will be there on the dot. If they are going to be more than ten minutes late they will call or text you. These people also respect their own time so don't be late for your own appointment. If you are, let the client know in good time. Treat people the way you want to be treated. I would say this is one of soundest indicators that you have a serious buyer. However, remember that sharks can be like this too. But you will be able to distinguish between them easily now.

People who are not serious will treat the matter that way. They will leave it until the last moment to inform you that, 'Unfortunately, due to a last minute thing', they are unable to make it. Over 80% of enquirers will cancel the appointment a day before. So how do you remedy this? One tactic is to phone the client a few days before and inform them that someone else connected to the business will be joining you on the day. Have that person call your client to confirm and say how keen they are to meet them. This puts pressure on the client to attend, because now they will be letting two people down if they decide not to come. It may also bring more seriousness to the table as you will be supported in your efforts to sell. But don't bring anyone who is not connected to the business, that would look daft.

However, if you can't get anyone else, then call the day before the meeting to confirm that the meeting is going ahead. I have found this to be a good litmus test since clients who are serious will say they'll be there and those who are not serious will cancel during that conversation.

2.2. The dress coded

I know many of us don't like to get up in the morning to don that special suit we only wore to a wedding, but this is the time to look the look.

Have you noticed that when someone is in uniform they immediately demand more respect than those around them? If an elevator gets stuck the guy wearing the IT suit will automatically be put in charge, although he may know nothing about lifts. We have been taught from an early age to respect a uniform. If you are approached by a man in a police uniform, you will immediately give him your undivided attention.

Your business suit is your uniform. It will demand respect. If your buyer turns up in baggy jeans, wearing sunglasses and a T-shirt it does not mean he is not a buyer. He is just not your ideal buyer. I have been in meetings where I am in a suit and the opposing person has chosen to go casual, they seem a little uptight (understandably), because they either did not know what to wear or did not know that it was important. This is where cultural behaviour comes into play. I once sold a construction company in Africa to a guy wearing torn trousers and smelling of compost. It was one of the highest prices paid at the time. However, in that culture and setting his dress was acceptable. He was a businessman who worked the work. If you find that your buyer is a new arrival to the country, then perhaps give them a break.

2.3. The date and time setter

This is a gem of an indicator. Let your prospective buyer choose a date and time to meet you. If they reverse the question, this means they are keen to meet. The world moves fast, if they have agreed to meet you, make it happen quickly. Don't take your time to get back to them but flip out your diary and give them a date before they decide to look at the next 'for sale' advert. Giving a buyer more time than they need means you have given them a reason for going elsewhere. Engaging a potential buyer means he now has work to do with you and cannot afford to look elsewhere. I find that a buyer's interest fades exponentially with time. Don't waste it.

Which day of the week? If your buyer says he can only meet you on the weekend he is an employee type of buyer as described above and is probably working for a company during the week. Either that or he has more important matters to attend to than meeting you during working hours.

I recommend that you **never** meet on a Sunday, especially if it is a first time meeting with the buyer. This is the only day of the week when everyone is more laid-back. It reminds most people of the relaxed Sundays they had off from school and they will appear to be not much interested. This is the Sunday mood syndrome and 9 out of 10 appointments set for a Sunday get cancelled due to family commitments.

The actual time of the meeting is also very important. The most productive time of day is the morning. A buyer who says he will be at your place in the morning is a serious prospect who has placed you in the top slot for the day. The afternoon is also good.

It is the evening time setters that you should be a little wary of. Life has its priorities and sub-routines and then there is 'free' time. If they have placed you that far down their 'to do' list you may be encroaching upon their 'free' time. Believe me when I say that the last thing you need is to meet someone who comes to you to talk about buying your business after a tiring day's work. Unless you both think it best, avoid scheduling meetings after 6pm.

The 'exact time' formula is a ploy used by some to make sure someone actually turns up on time. For example, if a meeting has been set for 1pm this subconsciously suggests that it will last for one hour. However, if you set the meeting for 12.45pm your buyer knows he has to be there by that time. Subconsciously, he sees the meeting ending at 1pm, lasting only 15 minutes, although he knows it will not end at that time. This was a tactic used by sales people making appointments. No one likes hard sales people who will stay for long periods of time. So they developed this solution to make people think that they would be there for only 15 minutes. Now who would not give someone 15 minutes of their time? The reality was, when they did turn up, they did the whole sales pitch and probably stayed for the full hour or even more.

Don't set the meeting time too early. No one wants to get out of bed unnecessarily early. Don't judge people too heavily on their time management either. Sometimes people have just had a really bad day. In these circumstances it is always better to re-arrange for another day. Never force a client to attend a meeting.

If you have been unfortunate enough to have been cancelled on, check why. If a prospective client pre-warned you then the situation is salvageable. If, however, there was no warning and your calls go unanswered, don't despair. They missed your opportunity. Move on to the next buyer. I have yet to find a true buyer who missed an appointment. Don't set another meeting unless you are sure that they will not be wasting your time again.

Now we have seen the types of buyers, let's look at how these potential buyers should be followed up, from their first enquiry to the point where you hand over the keys.

Chapter 6: The Follow Up

You have received your first enquiry and now need to follow it up. What is the best method? Here is the formula for getting the best results.

1. First contact

You must be jumping up and down, somebody is now actually interested enough in your business to send you an enquiry.

At this point you **must** have the following information about them, at the very least:

> The full name of the buyer
>
> Their phone number
>
> Their email address (if the enquiry came online).

Other useful details are their address and current occupation; what liquid capital they have to invest; and what their time frame is. Some websites allow you to ask questions of prospective buyers before they can send the enquiry form. However, asking too many questions may put buyers off.

One of the key ingredients of the follow up is **don't delay**. With every second that goes by your buyer is looking at more prospects.

I was interested in a business that was advertised for sale through a brokers. After the initial enquiry I was immediately contacted to sign an NDA before I could get any information. However, after signing it I received very little further information and no financial accounts. The brokers said they were waiting for information from the seller. In fact, they were sending a copy of my email to the seller, waiting for a reply, then sending the reply back to me. Each email was taking over a week to get answered. I finally got frustrated and lost interest.

2. NDA filter

The first contact should involve you sending an NDA (non-disclosure agreement) for adequate protection if you are going to be revealing names of customers or suppliers. An NDA is not a necessity but it has advantages. It will filter out students and people who then say that they are 'not the decision makers'. The NDA gets you the name of the person in charge. People who do not have the authority will avoid signing. The 'cons' of the NDA are that people may think you are a business broker not the actual owner who is placing the advert. You may want to clarify this in the follow-up. Another disadvantage is that some people don't like signing agreements before information has been exchanged.

Either email or call your prospect and politely request them to sign the agreement as a protection for both parties. You can email the NDA as an attachment and nowadays PDF documents can be signed digitally. Otherwise, ask them to scan or fax or post it back. The important thing is that you must tell them what they need to do next, clearly and concisely.

I have found that about one in every three enquirers do not reply. I suggest you follow up via a polite reminder after about a week. If calling, it is usual practice to first check that they received the NDA. It may have gone into their spam folder because of the attachment. Avoid sending links (such as YouTube links or directing them to your website), as these are picked up by spam filters. If you need to re-send it, ask them to send you a blank email first and then reply to it. Reply emails are usually not filtered out by spam filters since they are now 'trusted'.

One way of getting the number of enquiry replies up is to provide some information about the business at the same time as supplying the NDA. This little 'taster' works wonders if done correctly.

Print out the signed NDAs and keep them in a file.

3. The sale pack

The next information to send your prospect should repeat the information that was in the advert. This is so that your client will be satisfied that you are talking about the same business that was in the advert he replied to. It may sound ridiculous, but buyers sometimes feel that the business that was on offer may not be the one you are sending the information about. This is because so many businesses are bought and sold each day you can find that the business has either been sold or taken off the market.

New information also has to be provided. Send the market report, the business plan and the accounts. The two main elements are the business plan and accounts. If sending them by email keep it short and, since it is a reply, include the links to your website and video.

Then wait for at least three days. Avoid calling your prospect day and night. You don't want a restraining order made against you. Even if your prospect lives just down the road from you, never make un-arranged visits. In the same way, if your prospect suddenly turns up on your doorstep, be wary. If you are working from business premises with a policy where walk-in customers are welcome then that may be fine.

4. Enquirer goes silent

When an enquirer goes silent it is nothing to worry about. They are considering their options. Most people looking for businesses to buy are looking to keep their options open. For the serious buyer, it has less to do with finance than with the business. In most circumstances they may have given your sales pack to their accountant for an overview and the business plan to their banker to analyse. It takes about a week for replies.

Always be courteous and never force your prospect to make decisions on the phone. People don't like being put into a tight spot. If you do, they will fight out of it. People are not keen to take calls where they may be making a decision leading to payments of £100k+. Give people time and, to gauge their interest, ask via a text message or email. If they go unanswered it means they are thinking or have decided that it is not for them. That is fine.

Any follow up phone call you make, should just be to ask if they received your message. This puts much less emphasis on them making a decision about the sale and is much less stressful on the enquirer. People under less stress will be happier to talk to you and will also be more able to give you straight answers.

5. Handling multiple enquiries

'Sorry I will be unable to handle your enquiry as I am dealing with someone'. You must be bonkers! Unless you have received an offer on the business and are now exchanging monies, you must be able to handle multiple enquiries.

Most businesses will receive on average about 20 enquiries. If it is really well advertised you will get more. Make a folder on your computer and store all the enquiry details. Handle all the correspondence in a professional manner. Make notes on what has been said to each enquirer and what they have asked in return. The trail of correspondence is your lifeline and ultimately will decide on how well you progress with each one.

In all my sales, I made a habit of placing the enquirer's numbers on my mobile phone with their name and a reference to the business for sale. Whenever I received a call I would know who it was. This gave me a small advantage in handling the call.

What happens though, if you are lucky enough to find someone who now says, 'OK, I'm interested, what next'?

Chapter 7: Fish On A Hook

If you have ever been fishing you will know that selling a business is just like fishing. You have the equipment (your fishing net, bait and hooks), you cast your line (the advert) and finally the fish is on the hook.

A good buyer will wiggle as much as any good fish. This is where the prospective buyer is asking you questions about the business. Your replies need to be concise and to the point. Elaborate where necessary and don't ever avoid a question. The fish will just wiggle more.

Every business has black spots. This is the real world, it is expected. For every plus point you think you have, a weakness can be found in it. There is however a secret formula to the banter. A smart fisherman knows just how much to pull on the line and how much to let out the tension so that the fish does not snap it.

If you are in a position where the buyer may be wiggling out of being caught, you need to follow the smart fisherman's tactics. Do this by admitting to points that you know are true. Don't go over the top as that will lose you the deal. There is a fine line between saying too much and saying too little. Just like fishing, you pull too hard you snap the line, pull too little and the fish will get away.

So, how can you achieve this balance?

1.   The way buyers think

The answer is in your will and thoughts, and it is also hidden in the buyer's subconscious.

A little formula that I learnt along the way is that, if a buyer is really interested in your business, at one point they will have seen themselves running it. Be ready to answer any questions relating to how they would run the business. Some good ones are:

> How will I operate the business on a day to day basis without you?
>
> What happens in this instance?
>
> What would I need to do if that were to take place?

Will buyers speak to me once you are gone?

Passions are human emotions that we have little control over. The prospect of running a new business is as exciting to a business entrepreneur as a Christmas present is to a child. The only thing they're not doing is jumping up and down with the excitement. The serious buyer will display different indicators that you need to identify.

One key indicator is in their follow up. If, after giving them the information as outlined in the last chapter, they immediately ring or contact you to arrange an appointment that is a great indicator. They don't want to lose this opportunity. After all, you may have many other buyers out there.

Keeping to time and being smartly dressed are good, sound indicators. Some people can wear casual, but still look smart. Dressed to impress is about respecting and being respected back.

Buyers also want to be taken seriously. One sure way of getting their attention is to listen to them. There is no better way to gauge what they are thinking than letting them do the talking. Ask about their concerns and take feedback seriously.

Always look at the overall person and if they convey most of the good indicators that tells you that you have a good fish on the hook.

2.   Negotiating the final deal

You are almost at the end of your journey. You now have an interested buyer, or maybe even two, and there are offers on your business. A business offer needs to be looked at closely. It is not always about the price but the final deal.

2.1. Negotiating price

Contrary to public belief, price is the easiest of all negotiations. There is 'safety in numbers' and here a definite number is involved. If the main discussion point is only about price, this deal is yours to lose. Simply put, it is lost if they offer a price too small to consider. You have either not portrayed the real value of your business or they haven't seen it. It might be a case of their budget and what they are willing to spend.

Here are a few tips on negotiating the price:

- Don't negotiate on behalf of the buyer. This sounds strange but we all do it. How? You are asked by the buyer to name your lowest price, you quote the number you are expecting. You have just become your own enemy. If you are asked, always respond by asking them what they would be willing to offer. If no offer is forthcoming it shows that your buyer is biding their time.

- Never assume that an offer made is 'take it or leave it', even if the buyer says so. Experience has taught me that, unless your buyer is on a tight budget, they will negotiate to achieve success.

- A deal is a success for both buyer and seller – and we all want to succeed. This is why auctions are so popular. People bid against each other directly head to head. The highest bid is declared the winner. Remember, both sides want to win.

- Go for a reasonable price, don't expect all businesses to fetch millions.

- Don't be shy of saying no. Remember there are bigger and better fish out there.

2.2. Negotiating terms

Once the price is finalised the terms of the deal and how it will be executed matter very much.

At one point I was selling a printing franchise, the franchisee gave our franchise agreement to his solicitor to look at. The solicitor came back with suggestions on re-wording some of the terms. As a franchisor, we do not alter terms of our franchise agreements. What we did do, however, was draw up a separate agreement which clarified the terms and made the client happy. The price wasn't negotiated and we got the sale. Remember, there is always a way.

If you are offered a ridiculous price, and the buyer is testing you, one way forward is to reduce the offer of support or take out factors that were in the initial offer. Sometimes the client feels what is being taken out, does not monetarily mean much and this can drive the deal through.

You need to consider carefully any difficult terms that a prospect throws at you. Say, for instance, they ask you to provide extra services, such as after sale support. In most cases this is fine, but what if you were selling the business due to illness or moving location? Then look for someone who can provide the support and pay for it by charging the buyer. Don't let it be a deal-breaker, if you are getting a good price, absorb it!

In one deal, we were getting a very good price for a factory in London. The buyer was picky about the after sales support for a machine that needed trained supervision. We hired the manufacturer of the machine to give the support and we even hired outside help so the buyer was comfortable in his new surroundings. We could do this because we were getting a good price and we did not need to inform the buyer that this help was paid for. They received what was in the contract, they were happy, we were happy.

2.3. Legality

In every sale there are points that need to be straight from a legal standpoint. The business, any shares and other ownerships must be transferable. Any debts and business obligations need to be met before you transfer. Taxes and invoices need to be cleared, unless specified otherwise in the terms agreed. These points are easily met by using a good solicitor to oversee the sale process.

Some sales contain terms where payments are released at certain times or after particular actions or events. For instance, on signing a certain percentage is released, with a further payment on receiving ownership titles and a final payment on completion of training or after a certain period of time.

These payments need to be well-documented. The usual process is whenever a 'credit' is given a 'guarantee' needs to be in place. This can avoid the costly business of pursuing late or non payers. Do make sure that you cover any later payments, unless you are happy to kiss them goodbye. Having said this, not all people are bad payers or have bad intentions, sometimes times makes them so. You, however, should not have to deal with that.

I once sold a print franchise and gave 'credit' to the buyer who seemed quite reputable and honest. I did not request a guarantee. Only the initial payments were made and then, to avoid further payments, the buyer decided to litigate matters in the hope that I would write off the final payment. Given the opportunity people will try anything, especially in hard times. Not everyone is dishonest but be wary.

If you are offered an 'earn-out', where you get paid out of the person working the business, it is advisable to take a reasonable deposit up front. Keep a charging order on the assets and draw up a schedule for payments. Remember, giving credit can mean headaches later on.

When in doubt, hire a solicitor who specialises in business sales.

3. Closing the sale

Now you are truly out of the woods and the sale is approaching completion.

All that remains to be done is to sign the agreements. Read the terms carefully if you are not the party who has prepared the contract or, better still, get it looked at by a professional.

If the sale is a large one, you may have several people on the day to read the terms by each party's accountants, solicitors and bankers. If all looks well, it is a success for both parties, sign the documents.

There should always be three copies: 'One for the master (you), one for the dame (buyer) and one for the little boy who lives down the lane (solicitor).' Make sure that third copy is stored by a third party or a witness if a solicitor is not working on the deal.

4. Taking payment

Large payments, or payments made during the signing, are usually made by cheque. However, in today's electronic age, TT (telegraphic transfer) payments can be made via a laptop during the signing ceremony.

In the UK electronic payments of less than £100,000 are instantaneous, larger payments can take between 2 hours and a day to process. If your bank account has not received large amounts of money in the past, you may get a call from your bank to confirm what the remittance is for. You may be asked to let them see your sale contract to avoid money laundering. In most cases there is hardly ever a hitch.

Bank financing is more time consuming, especially if the funds are not already in place. Always request a decent upfront payment if you have any doubts and follow the rule about getting a guarantee in place for future payments. Even if it means getting them to sign a personal guarantee, although, in my opinion, these do not really mean a lot.

If a bank is making the payments, the deal is best done at the buyer's or seller's bank. They will keep a record of the documents and payments will be confirmed by them then and there.

Congratulations you have done it!

Chapter 8: After Sale

Well done!

Your business has been sold and now you can think about going on that planned holiday. Although this is the ideal scenario because of the terms of the agreement it may not be time to book the flights just yet.

1.   What to expect

The new owners may well have asked for support that will require more of your input than you anticipated. This is normal.

After the sale it is a courtesy that the seller provide 'extra' help to the new owners to help them settle in. There are many small secrets about the business that sellers don't reveal before the final sale stamp. Once the business is not theirs they open up completely and it is always a good idea to meet up with the new owner and talk over a hot cup of coffee or tea. After this, unless there are other covenants in the agreement, then say goodbye and book your holiday.

2.   Covenants on sale terms

I was a consultant to a factory sale in which the buyer wanted more technical support than the previous owner could give. As purely an investor his technical knowledge was minimal, to say the least. This was not known until after the sale was completed!

In any sale there should be ample communication about support and training. In this instance, the buyer made the mistake of pouncing on the deal. The seller had reduced the price because he wanted a walk-in, walk-out deal and would not provide any support. Unfortunately, this was not explained properly. Part-money was exchanged, but now the new buyer was looking at a non-working factory floor. We were in a tough sales situation.

Fortunately a local technician who could provide the support and training required came to the rescue. The cost was covered by the seller, equating to no more than a parking fine for not seeing the obvious.

3. What next?

Research suggests that people who do not retire live longer and lead healthier lives. The brain keeps active and so mental health remains more stable.

Find your next project. Don't stop. Look for a business to buy and, most important of all, enjoy life and whatever you decide to do, do it with all the **will** and conviction you have.

Have a successful future.